Explore and Draw

WHALES

DRAWING AND READING

Gare Thompson

ROURKE PUBLISHING
www.rourkepublishing.com

Editor: Penny Dowdy
Art Direction: Cheena Yadav (Q2AMedia)
Designer: Suzena Samuel, Ravinder Kumar (Q2AMedia)
Illustrator: Prithwiraj Samat
Picture researcher: Rajeev Kumar Parmar (Q2AMedia)

Picture credits:
t=top b=bottom c=centre l=left r=right
Cover: Rod Kaye/Istockphoto.
Back Cover: Rod Kaye/Istockphoto, Roessler Carl/Photolibrary, Tischenko Irina/Shutterstock, Cretolamna/Shutterstock, Nathan Jones/Istockphoto, David Lewis/Istockphoto, Malou Leontsinis/ Shutterstock, Radoslav Stoilov/Shutterstock, Close Encounters Photography/Shutterstock, CTR Photos/ Shutterstock.
Title Page: Clara/Shutterstock, Brett Atkins/ Shutterstock, Bocos Benedict/Shutterstock, Cbpix/ Shutterstock, Four Oaks/Shutterstock, Alexey Stiop/ Shutterstock, Richard A. McGuirk/Shutterstock, Jeremy Wee/Shutterstock, Mana Photo/ Shutterstock, Phillip Hobbs Andresen/Shutterstock, Andreas Meyer/Shutterstock, Christopher Meder Photography/Shutterstock, Eky Studio/Shutterstock.
Insides: Clara/Shutterstock, Brett Atkins/ Shutterstock, Bocos Benedict/Shutterstock, Cbpix/ Shutterstock, Four Oaks/Shutterstock, Alexey Stiop/ Shutterstock, Richard A. McGuirk/Shutterstock, Jeremy Wee/Shutterstock, Mana Photo/

Shutterstock, Phillip Hobbs Andresen/Shutterstock, Andreas Meyer/Shutterstock, Christopher Meder Photography/Shutterstock, Eky Studio/Shutterstock. Clara/Shutterstock, Brett Atkins/Shutterstock, Bocos Benedict/Shutterstock, Cbpix/Shutterstock, Four Oaks/Shutterstock, Alexey Stiop/Shutterstock, Richard A. McGuirk/Shutterstock, Jeremy Wee/ Shutterstock, Mana Photo/Shutterstock, Phillip Hobbs Andresen/Shutterstock, Andreas Meyer/ Shutterstock, Christopher Meder Photography/ Shutterstock, Eky Studio/Shutterstock: 4-24, Ferderic B/Shutterstock: 6, Chris Cutler/NOAA Photo Library: 7, Reinhard Dirscherl/Photolirbary: 10, Andreas Meyer/123RF: 11, NOAA Photo Library: 14, Gerard Soury/Photolibrary: 15, Nico Tondini/Robert Harding Travel/Photolibrary: 18, Markabond/Shutterstock: 19.

Q2AMedia Art Bank: Cover, Back Cover, Title Page, 4-5, 8-9, 12-13, 16-17, 20-21.

Library of Congress Cataloging-in-Publication Data

Becker, Ann, 1965 Oct. 6-
Whales: explore and draw / Gare Thompson.
p. cm. – (Explore and draw)
Includes index.
ISBN 978-1-61590-253-8 (hard cover)
ISBN 978-1-61590-493-8 (soft cover)
1. Whales in art–Juvenile literature. 2. Drawing–Technique–Juvenile literature.
I. Title. II. Title: Explore and draw.
NC825.A4B43 2009
743'.8962913334–dc22
2009021617

Rourke Publishing
Printed in the United States of America, North Mankato, Minnesota
033010
033010LP

www.rourkepublishing.com - rourke@rourkepublishing.com
Post Office Box 643328 Vero Beach, Florida 32964

Contents

Technique   4

Meet the Whales   6

Draw a Killer Whale   8

Toothed Whales   10

Draw a Sperm Whale   12

Baleen Whales   14

Draw a Humpback Whale   16

Dolphins and Porpoises   18

Draw a Bottlenose Dolphin   20

Glossary   22

Index   23

Websites to Visit   24

Technique

Are you ready to draw whales? First, you need to understand the basic form of a whale. There are certain shapes you can use to sketch the whale in **proportion**. Using a backline will help. The backline is the whale's back.

1

Start by drawing a long, curved backline. Use it as your guide. Then draw a large oval around it. The oval will form the whale's body. Add a smaller square for the whale's head.

2

Draw two small triangles on each side of the whale's body. These are the fins. Add a **crescent** across the end of the backline for the whale's tail. Draw a small circle for the whale's eye.

3

Add light guidelines to connect the parts of the whale's body. Round the whale's head to make it look more realistic. Now you have the complete shape of a whale.

4

Draw a long, thin line for the mouth. Add detail to the tail and the fins. Smooth the lines of the whale.

5

Use light and dark tones to **shade** the drawing. Your drawing will be more interesting.

Meet the Whales

Whales can be found in every ocean, but they are not fish. Whales are **mammals**. They breathe air through an opening in the top of their head. This is called a **blowhole**. There are two **species**, or kinds of whales: toothed whales and **baleen** whales.

Toothed Whales

As you would expect, toothed whales have teeth. They use their teeth for hunting and protection. They eat mostly squid and fish. Toothed whales have only one blowhole. Dolphins, sperm whales, and killer whales are toothed whales.

The killer whale is the largest member of the whale family.

Dolphins and porpoises are part of the whale family.

Baleen Whales

Baleen whales do not have teeth. Instead, they have baleen plates in their jaw. These plates look like combs. Water pours through the baleen plates, leaving the food behind. Some baleen whales eat **krill**, tiny shrimp-like creatures. Others eat fish. Baleen whales have two blowholes. The blue whale, right whale, and humpback whale are baleen whales.

Whale Hunting and Watching

People have hunted whales for hundreds of years. Whale parts were used to make oil, perfume, and even buggy whips. After years of hunting, many kinds of whales became nearly **extinct**. Very few were left. Countries passed laws to keep whales safe. Today, people go on whale watches. They take pictures of whales instead of hunting them.

Draw a Killer Whale

The killer whale has a sleek, streamlined body.

1 Draw a long, curved backline to form the center of the body. Add a large oval around the middle of the backline for the body. Draw a large circle for the head. Add a very small circle to the front of the head for the nose.

2 Draw three triangles to each side of the body for the fins. Add a crescent shape to the back of the body for the tail. Add a small circle for the eye. Connect the body with light guidelines.

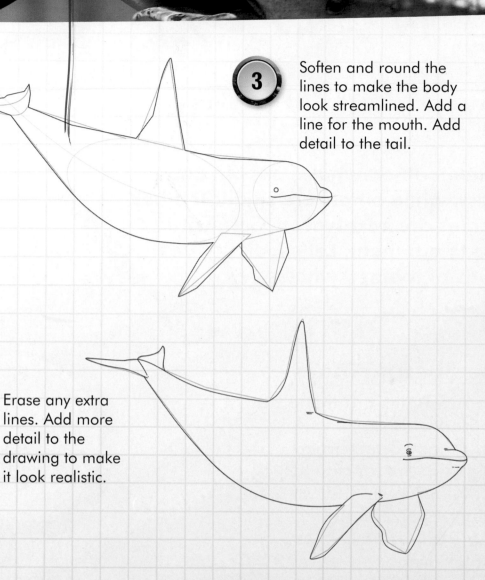

3 Soften and round the lines to make the body look streamlined. Add a line for the mouth. Add detail to the tail.

4 Erase any extra lines. Add more detail to the drawing to make it look realistic.

5 Shade the whale using its special black and white markings.

9

Toothed Whales

Some toothed whales are big and scary, while others are small. Toothed whales are **carnivores**. Carnivores like to eat meat. Let's look at three kinds of toothed whales.

The Sperm Whale

Sperm whales are the largest toothed whales. They have giant teeth. Their brain weighs about 20 pounds (9.1 kilograms). Their heart weighs over 276 pounds (125.2 kilograms). These whales are found all over the world. In the 1800s, people hunted them for their oil. The oil was used to make candles, soap, and machine oil. Today, laws protect these large whales.

The whale in the famous book *Moby Dick* is a sperm whale.

In the Middle Ages, people sold narwhal tusks as unicorn horns.

The Narwhal

Narwhal whales are called the unicorn of the oceans. They have a **tusk**, which looks like a unicorn's horn. Tusks can grow to 7-10 feet (2-3 meters) long. Narwhals are found in Arctic waters. They eat fish. Narwhals make deep dives. They can dive up to 2,400 feet (800 meters) several times a day.

The Killer Whale

Killer whales are also known as orcas. They have a black back and a white chest and sides. They look like large dolphins. Killer whales have no natural **predators**. People feared these whales for years, but they do not eat humans. Killer whales live in **pods**. Pods are family groups of 5-6 related animals. Killer whales use clicks and whistles to talk to each other.

Draw a Sperm Whale

Sperm whales have big square heads.

1 Draw a curved backline as the center of a large rectangle for the body. Add a triangle to one end of the rectangle for the whale's rear. Draw a crescent shape for the tail.

2 Add two triangles to each side of the body for the fins. Draw a small circle for the eye.

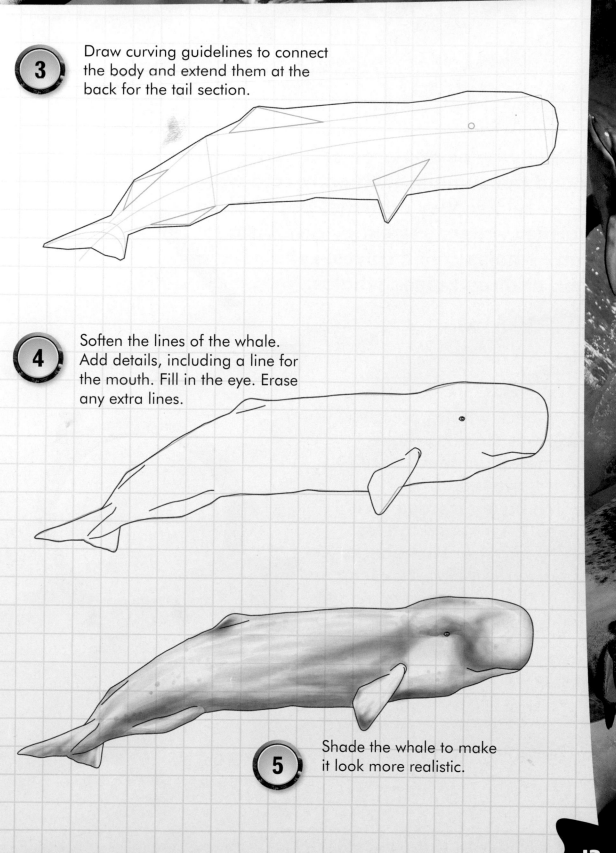

3 Draw curving guidelines to connect the body and extend them at the back for the tail section.

4 Soften the lines of the whale. Add details, including a line for the mouth. Fill in the eye. Erase any extra lines.

5 Shade the whale to make it look more realistic.

Baleen Whales

Baleen whales are large and gentle. Most spend the summer feeding in cold waters. In the winter they **migrate**, or travel, to warmer waters. Here they give birth to baby whales called calves. Let's look at three baleen whales.

Singing Whales

Humpback whales are also known as singing whales. The male humpback sings, but no one is sure why. People have recorded their songs. Their songs can last for 30 minutes. Humpbacks can also do tricks. They leap out of the ocean like acrobats. This is called **breaching**.

Whales may breach to warn of danger.

A right whale is about the same size as a bus.

Big Blue

Blue whales are even bigger than dinosaurs. They are the largest mammals to have ever lived. They eat about 4 tons (3.6 metric tons) of food a day. They can eat up to 4 million krill each day! Blue whales actually look blue under water. These whales were hunted almost to extinction. Today, they are an **endangered species**.

Right Whales

Right whales are rare whales known for their large heads. Their bodies are mostly black. Whale hunters named these whales the *right* whales to hunt and kill. So these whales almost died out. Today, these whales are also an endangered species.

Draw a Humpback Whale

The humpback whale has a stocky body with humps along its back. It also has large front flippers and a knobby head. Its long black and white tail fin can be up to a third of its body length.

1 Draw a curved backline to form the center of the whale's body. Add a large oval around the middle of the backline. Draw a smaller oval around the back and a small circle around the front of the backline. These shapes will form the body of the whale.

2 Draw two large triangles below the body for the large front flippers. Add a smaller triangle for the top fin. Draw a crescent shape to form the tail and a small circle for the eye. Connect the shapes with light guidelines.

3 Soften the lines to make the body look more natural. Add detail to the tail.

 4 Draw more detail to the face, eye, and flippers. Add a wavy line for the mouth. Erase any extra lines.

 5 Shade the whale and draw in more detail to add interest.

17

Dolphins and Porpoises

Most people are surprised to learn that dolphins and porpoises are part of the whale family. These two mammals are alike but also different. Dolphins have a beak, while porpoises do not. Let's look at two dolphins and one porpoise.

The Pink River Dolphin

Pink river dolphins live in the Amazon River in South America. These dolphins use **echolocation** to communicate. Their whistles and clicks bounce off objects underwater. The sounds create echoes that help the dolphins find food. Today, the **habitat** of the pink river dolphins is being destroyed. They are an endangered species.

Scientists think pink river dolphins are the smartest of the dolphins.

The Bottlenose Dolphin

Bottlenose dolphins live in pods. Pods can range from fifteen animals to hundreds. Bottlenose dolphins work as a team to hunt for fish. They herd the fish into small circles and then take turns having a meal.

The Harbor Porpoise

Harbor porpoises are one of the smallest of the ocean mammals. Their bodies are small and stocky. Harbor porpoises usually live in harbors in coastal areas. They feed on small fish. Their enemies are their cousins, the orcas, and white sharks.

Bottlenose dolphins are friendly and easy to train.

Draw a Bottlenose Dolphin

Bottlenose dolphins are the most common dolphins. They are called bottlenose because of their short, stubby beaks.

1 Draw a curved backline. Add a large oval in the middle, a circle at one end for the head, and a smaller circle at the other end for the tail. Draw a very small circle in front of the head for the beak.

2 Draw light guidelines to connect the shapes and form the basic body. Add triangles on both sides of the body for the fins. Draw a crescent shape for the tail.

3 Soften and round the lines to make the dolphin look more natural. Add a small circle for the eye. Expand the tail.

4 Add detail to the beak and eye. Erase any extra lines.

5 Shade the dolphin. The tips of the fins and tail should be the darkest.

Glossary

baleen (buh-LEEN): comb-like whalebone in the jaw of some whales; used to filter food

blowhole (BLOH-hohl): an opening on top of the head of a whale; used to take in air

breaching (BREECH-ing): leaping from the water

carnivores (KAHR-nuh-vohrz): animals that eat meat

crescent (KRES-uhnt): a thing shaped like the moon when you can only see a thin, curved part of it

echolocation (ek-oh-loh-KAY-shun): when dolphins listen to the echoes of the sounds they make underwater to communicate and find food

endangered species (en-DAYN-juhrd SPEE-sheez): a group of animals or plants that are at risk of becoming extinct

extinct (ek-STINGKT): no longer existing

habitat (HAB-uh-tat): a place where an animal or plant naturally lives and grows

krill (KRIL): tiny, shrimp-like animals

mammals (MAM-uhlz): warm-blooded animals that have a backbone and produce milk to feed their young

migrate (MIGH-grayt): moving from one place to another

pods (PODZ): families or groups of sea animals

predators (PRED-uh-turz): animals that kill other animals for food

proportion (pruh-POHR-shun): the relation of one thing to another with regard to size

shade (SHAYD): to make part of a drawing darker than the rest

species (SPEE-sheez): a group of animals or plants that share many qualities

tusk (TUSK): a long, pointed tooth that sticks out of the mouth

Index

baleen whale(s) - 6, 7, 14, 15

blue whale(s) - 7, 15

bottlenose dolphins - 19, 20, 21

breaching - 14

dolphins - 6, 18, 19

harbor porpoises - 19

humpback whales - 7, 15, 16, 17

killer whale(s) - 8, 9, 11

krill - 7

Moby Dick - 10

narwhals - 11

orcas - 11, 19

pink river dolphins - 18

pods – 11, 19

porpoises - 18, 19

right whale(s) - 7, 15

sperm whale(s) - 10, 12, 13

toothed whales - 6, 10

whale watches - 7

Websites to Visit

www.acsonline.org
Gives information about whales and the whale family, including organizations that work to save whales.

http://www.whales.org.za/
Explores the world of whales. Enjoy the slide show, facts, news, and information about whales and the whale family.

http://www.pbs.org/wnet/nature/episodes/humpback-whales/
Discover all you want to know about humpback whales: their songs, habitats, diets, and physical characteristics.

About the Author
Gare Thompson has written over 200 children's books. He has also taught elementary school. He lives in Massachusetts with his wife. During the summer, he and his family like to go on whale watches. Whales are one of his favorite animals. He has written several books on whales and whaling.

About the Illustrator
Prithwiraj Samat has illustrated a number of children's books. He has a Bachelor in Visual Arts. Prithwiraj draws primarily realistic art. He loves drawing the world around him. Prithwiraj lives with his family in New Delhi. He has been working for Q2A Media for one year.